THE SHORE OF THE UNKNOWN

*For Bennett Elizabeth
My very Best
Don*

Other works by Donald J. Young

NOVELS
> *The Reunion* (New International Library, 1961)
> *The Lion's Share,* A Story of the Battle of the Bulge
> (Avranches Press, 1998, Fourth Edition)

POETRY
> Early poems—not included in this book—appeared in *Epoch, Furioso, Western Review, The Black Mountain Press, Dark Tower, Sundaze,* and *Coastlines.*

THE SHORE OF THE UNKNOWN

POEMS BY
DONALD J. YOUNG

AVRANCHES PRESS
Aptos, California

Published by Avranches Press
1700 Cheryl Way
Aptos, CA 95003
USA

Front cover photograph: *Moon, Cliff, and Wave*
Chris Bratt
110 First Avenue
Santa Cruz, CA 95062

Cover and text design, photo manipulation: Phyllis Wright

Author photograph: Greg Pio

Copyright © 1998
All rights reserved
Library of Congress Catalog Number 98-90890
ISBN 0-9625886-2-8

TO VIVIANE
For all her love and support

We see the world piece by piece, as the sun, the moon, the animal, the tree; but the whole, of which these are the shining part, is the soul.

—Ralph Waldo Emerson, *The Over-Soul*

FOREWORD

In writing the poems for *The Shore of the Unknown*, I was indebted to the work of Rumi, the Persian poet (1207–1273), whose poems revealed a language of the spirit which helped me understand certain experiences I had.

I want to thank my friend, Harry Card, who gave me many creative suggestions on how to improve the poems.

Phyllis Wright was very considerate and innovative in preparing the book for publication.

I am very grateful to the photographer, Chris Bratt, for his gracious permission to use, for the front cover, his beautiful photo, *Moon, Cliff, and Wave*. His magnificent photographs of mountains, streams, and the sea, have been shown in many exhibitions in Santa Cruz, throughout California, and recently in the Boston area. He reveals in his work an original view of nature, which resembles expressionistic painting at its best.

From THE SHORE OF THE UNKNOWN, pg. 15

The soul is a burning desire...from *Reverence for Life* by Albert Schweitzer.

The eye of the soul...adapted from a passage in Marsilio Ficino's *The Planets Within*.

The soul is a shell...adapted from a passage in *Man is not Alone,* by Abraham Joshua Heschel.

THE SHORE OF THE UNKNOWN

The Shore of the Unknown 15
If Only I Could Write 16
Poems Written After Reading Rumi
    A Halfway Poem 17
    I Didn't Write a Poem 18
    My Friends Grow Cold 20
    Forget Your Hatred 21
    Even If You Don't Believe 23
    Don't Drink 24
My Friend's Poetry 26
Every Once in a While 28
I Was a Scholar Once .30
When Young 32
Three Famous Men 34
Out of the Closet 38
I Find It Odd 40
The War 42
On the Dead 44
On Dreams 47
Understanding 49
We Want to Be Free 50
Jesus, How They Treated You 52

The Shore of the Unknown

Was it the sun's fault
or the opening
of my heart
with the uni-
versal thread
that brought forth,
from the soul singers,
this torrent of words?—

*The soul is a burn-
ing desire to breathe
in the world of light.*

*The eye of the soul
is the gateway to
the imagined world.*

*The soul is a shell
wherein we hear
the murmur of the waves
from the unknown shore.*

If Only I Could Write

If only I could write
just what I feel,
instead of thinking,
now, I'm writing a poem.

I'd write about
that rare technician
who pierced my heart
with a subtle thread,
and kept it beating.

And *then* I'd write about
that woman in blue,
her cap enlivened by
a lamp of gold,
who bandaged my wound
with air, which is—
the mystics say—
the breath that makes
the earth unfold.

Poems Written After Reading Rumi

A Halfway Poem

Although I only made it
halfway through
my poem of love,
I thought that maybe,
in a halfway flight
into myself,
I might incite
others to let
the bird of life,
as Rumi says,
begin to beat
its wings
and fly to love.

I Didn't Write a Poem

I didn't write
a poem today,
I didn't have
the feel for it,—
as if I'd smoked
some rare hashish
and didn't need
to do a thing.

My soul, approving,
then replied, "It's not
too late to go on
doing nothing now.
And when your friends complain that *fame
is the spur,* etcetera,
just tell them that I,
your soul,
have come back home
from the bookstalls
and lecture halls
and those exotic
lands you traveled to—
where you imprisoned me.

Just tell your friends
that now, like Keats,
we'll feast our eyes
on the sea,
where Rumi says
we all lived once,
and after life
we will reside,
where love en-
shrouds us all."

My Friends Grow Cold

My friends grow cold
when I speak
of the mystic
who sings
of the glory
of listening
with the inner ear.

"Be quiet," Rumi says.
"Don't speak of money,
household goods,
or jealousy
or lust for power."

My friends, meanwhile,
object, their talk
like static;
I leave them only
to clear my head,
so the soul can hear
the waves repeat-
ing their endless
sermon on the
furthest shore.

Forget Your Hatred

Forget your hatred
for the neighbor
whose branches reach
across the fence
to strangle
your favor-
ite rose.

Forget your hatred
for those on the pol-
itical Right or Left;
forget to rage
over views that mir-
ror the dark
side of your own.

Forget ideas
that paralyze
the heart.
Printing them
will not appease
your enemy.
Print your feelings,
like Rumi,
on the air.

Persuade your children
to live for stillness,
exchanging love
which the air
carries like seeds.

If still you want a song,
record the music
that was sung
in Eden,
before the airs
of nothingness
hounded us
in the nightmare woods.

Listen to the songbirds
who dwell in air, —
without ignoring
the earth,
giving us that
reassurance
of ecstatic sounds,
which echo from
the canyon
of living souls.

Even If You Don't Believe

Even if you don't believe
you have a soul,
take Rumi's word.
Either get wasted
on the wine
that is offered
or let it go.
Play dead or breathe
the air from the
crystal palace
on the invis-
ible shore.

Don't Drink

Don't drink what your parents
put on the table,
pouring their wine
out of those lovely
old decanters;
or what your friend drinks,
however chummy he appears
at the noisy bar.

Don't drink what your neigh-
bor does, though adver-
tised on all the signs;
or what the poli-
tician urges
from his public post.

Don't drink what the god-
dess showgirl does,
inviting you with her breasts
to try her brand;
don't even drink
what your lover does,
though you pour
her wine for her.

Drink only that wine
which stirs the soul,
and when you're drunk
on that peerless beverage,
banish thought,
which kills all
ecstasy,
and settle back
immobilized
by wine, with only
your soul as a drink-
ing companion.

My Friend's Poetry

I'm always amazed
by the images, as fresh
as morning air,
which pour from my
friend's head
in such profusion
that they almost
drown his work.

"Stay close to earth,"
he says. "Make songs
to flowers, stones,
the mountains and lakes,
which are inside of us.
See nature first,
and since there is
no heaven, never try
to reach beyond the stars."

But thinking this way, I feel,
demeans the glory
of seeing the world
with the Other eye—

which is, the mystics claim,
the only way to leave
the prison of the self
and come again to
the soul's residence.

Every Once in a While

Every once in a while,
as I leaf through
this massive book
of poems
from all nations,
I find a poet
who doesn't go on,
like the others,
about the flowers
that enhance the air;
who doesn't write of
whistling nightingales;
who doesn't compose
elegies to glassy
lakes and sky-
capped hills.

This poet shows us
how the flowers
enhance the air;
how birds
propel themselves
across the sky;
and *how* the glassy lakes
and snow-capped hills
are blessed.

Then taking in the sound
of his great notes,
we hold a shell
to the ear, and hear
from the soul's castle
miraculous melodies.

I Was a Scholar Once

I was a scholar once
and rambled on
with friends about
an arcane book,
with symbols from afar,
which I would strain
to comprehend.

Then later on I gave
the book to my friend:
a priest as round
as any friar,
with glasses leaning
on his nose like
Schubert's—who loved
Spinoza, Plato,
Martin Buber.

"I didn't understand
your book," he said,
his hand upon my neck,
"for years ago I had
to leave the castle
of the intellect."
And then he talked
of friends and kind-
ness and his care
for other men.

Ashamed of my book
and changed by his touch,
I saw that all
my friend had left
from his mind's work
was his love for me.

When Young

When young I went
on a journey,
and, drafted by lot,
I was shipped by sea
to a war, where my
fellows were slaughtered
in a day,
and where as a prisoner
I was laid in a tomb-
like cell, which was
demolished by the pilots
of my country, who
buried me
in the dust.

Since then I won't go
any place unless I
know where I'm going—

I'll head for
diviner air
and, knowing
where I'm going,
I'll free myself of
the known world ticking
like a bomb.
I'll feel the sacred
life enfolding me.

Three Famous Men

By chance at the college
where I taught,
I met three famous men.
The first was Eliot,
who took an empty
seat at the table,
which was the custom
in the dining hall.

While bending down
to take his place
he seemed to hang
above us like
"the aged eagle"
he said he was,
whose wreathed eyes
made him appear
the oldest man
I'd ever seen.

His sleep had been disturbed, he said,
by a blast
of dynamite
that cleared the way
for a campus hall.

I figured then that he
was thinking of his nights
as air raid warden
on a roof,
hearing the blast of
"the dove with flicker-
ing tongue,"
which dropped
its deadly load
on dying London.

I met the aging Frost
who kindly read my verse;
and later at a dance
appeared to me
like any farmer out
on Saturday night—
his sculptured visage
bronzed by the sun
like a patina
on an ancient bust.

Observing the dancers
in the crowded barn,
Frost must've thought
the dance, with its
mythic beat,

emerged from a primal
source, to enter
his earthy soul.

The third was Einstein
who talked to us at night—
in baggy pants, old
tennis shoes, and
with those large
and soulful eyes
that had looked into
the heart of light.

He laughed—a nervous
tic, while shaking
like a mop,
his rumpled hair.
"We must be careful
with the bomb," he said,
"or else we'll blow
up everything;"
and pushing back
his white wild locks,
he burst out with
an echoing laugh.

These famous men
reminded me
that the souls of men
are hidden in
the sea of souls,
and give no hint
of greatness in
their common acts
of courtesy.

Out of the Closet

So many men
are coming out
of the closet,
or being brought out
by their enemies.
I thought of
Billy Strayhorn
of the *lush music*
the Duke took credit for;
and Cole too
of the dark song,
"Love For Sale";
and Hart with his
"This Can't Be Love."

I later learned
that Thomas Mann
was serious
when his Aschenbach,
in Venice, looked
with longing
on the Grecian
bronze-skinned
boy at the beach.

I also heard from friends
that Goethe loved
to swim the livelong day
with naked German lads.

I thought of Bobby Dent,
the neighbor boy
we ridiculed at home—
who drowned himself
in our canal.
Would he have
been redeemed
if he had known
that he was *one*
with those dis-
tinguished men
who loved a man?

Such musings
made me think
that after the closet
is emptied of guilt,
and loneliness,
disease and death,
we should all
just let anyone alone
who feels love
pulling them
like a river.

I Find It Odd

I find it odd
that everyone—
at some time
or other—takes
a moral stand.

Leaders who smile
and cheat us
while they smile
will talk in-
cessantly
of truth.

The tyrants who sub-
jugate the weak
with a brutal arm
have moments of doubt.

Even the bitter
soldiers—once the
war is lost—
believe it's better
not to go on butch-
ering the enemy's
women and children.

I find it odd
that even the primal
shadow-man
in all of us
cowers before
its image
in the holy glass.

The War

The war, we came to
think, turned all of us
to stones, as hard
as bullet shells.
For seeing what we
had to see,
we feigned that
no such war occurred.

Then after all that blood,
a rose outside our room
waved many flags
of white pink buds;
the hyacinth beguiled us
with its perfumed lazi-
ness; the columbine
put down its blooms
like markers on a grave;
and all the flowers
that blossomed on
the fields of death,
clamored for peace.

I heard the echoing song
of one who never
blamed me in the
time of war for dis-
enchanting her.—

Until at last, after
all the dumb dog days,
I could lay down
a ring of tears,
like a wreath,
on all the stones
that we'd become.

On the Dead

I often wonder why
the dead keep
posing questions,
which make us feel
we've let them down.

Once and for all
I wish they'd
let us alone.
I try to speak
well of them.
So why do they
keep harping
on our im-
perfections?
Is that the only
thing which makes
them feel alive?

I wonder why
they lie so still,
sleeping through
their mean re-
criminations,

making us feel
we've never been
good at anything,
bullying us about
the hollowness
of our lives?

I still distrust their
moral certainty,
their hypo-
critical silence
about *their* failures.

Nearing the end,
when we enter
the soul's country,
the dead laugh,
saying we should keep
our view of the ab-
surdity of life,
though they have faith
and claim an after-
life for themselves.

Well, I'm through
with this:
I'm actually thinking
now like the dead, —
longing for
a heaven of the mind,
where we, though flawed
in this life,
will succeed
in all things.

On Dreams

I'd like to think
my dreams provide
a key that will
unlock my mind.

But mine are ob-
vious: I'm late
for a rendezvous;
I come on stage
with no lines to say;
I'm lost in a desert
with no idea
which way to turn.

In one recurring
dream—so obvious—
I'm cleaning a skull
and polishing
the bald dome
with a dirty rag;
And then I know—
the skull is mine.

Whenever now I dream
of naked ladies,
I always offer them
a robe,

and then escort them
to the ocean
where they, disappear-
ing, rise on the foam,
like Venus
from her shell.

I hope, in my after-
life, I'll have
a dream of earth
in which I'll live
outrageously,
with a love
on every wind,
while from my
polished skull
will burst
a flourish
of wild spring buds.

Understanding

When a friend is mis-
understood
he is locked in-
side, sans chains;
when a friend mis-
understands
he winds the chains
about his friend,
like Minos' snake.

When we are under-
stood and under-
stand, we're free
of the rattling bonds;
and the light
over the sea is
blinding, and
we hear a voice
from the deepest
watery cavern where
a god is hiding.

We Want to Be Free

We want to be free
of the longing to
be esteemed;
to make a name
in the world;
to be admired for
know-how;
and of course—
above all—
to be loved.

Such longing makes us
ill at ease,
even with beauty
calling us
in the name of flowers
to forget
these useless things
we long for
just because the others
live by them.

We're never at ease
even with one sure
lover in the house
whom we make love to,
and—miracle of mir-
acles—we go on loving.

The mystic says,
"Empty the head;
stop thinking;
stop comparing your-
self to anyone;
just be quiet
for a while!"

Jesus, How They Treated You

Jesus, how they treated
you, saying you weren't
human—placing you far
above us, even saying
that you existed
before Time.

Thus foolish men
could mock
"the unbelievers"
who follow you
in any other way.

All you really asked
was that we love
the woman at the well;
the child molester;
murderer;
the men who beat
their children and wives;
and even German men
who burned
their Jewish daughters.

Christ, how hard it is
to love.
Teach me to hold on
beyond grief and hate
for man's incessant
heartlessness,
until my spirit,
drunk with the wine of joy,
dances along
with You to the long
invisible corridor
of love.

Critical comments on Don Young's novel
THE LION'S SHARE

I liked THE LION'S SHARE. It rings true. Only someone who was there could have written it. —JOHN TOLAND
Battle: The Story of the Bulge and The Last Hundred Days

I've read THE LION'S SHARE practically in one sitting with considerable admiration. The book is wonderfully readable.
—PAUL FUSSELL
The Great War and Modern Memory

I enjoyed THE LION'S SHARE thoroughly. It most resembles impressionistic painting: the colors make a picture for you. The book succeeds admirably.
—OLIVER PATTON, Brigadier General, Retired
The Silent Snow

I enjoyed reading THE LION'S SHARE (good title, too). It stirred lots of memories of World War II. —PAGE SMITH
A People's History of the United States

THE LION'S SHARE resembles a miniature *Catch–22* and *Slaughterhouse Five*, both rolled into one.... Brilliant, incisive, and bitingly ironic.... An original look at warfare.
—MORTON MARCUS
Pages from a Scrapbook of Immigrants

Hats off to a fine war novel—one of the best—right up there with O'Brien's *Going After Cacciato*. The surreal, absurd aspects of combat and imprisonment are wonderfully rendered. —ROBERT PETERSON
Leaving Taos

**To order THE LION'S SHARE, send $10.00
(which includes tax and shipping) to:
AVRANCHES PRESS
1700 Cheryl Way
Aptos, CA 95003**

DONALD J. YOUNG

Don Young became interested in fiction at Princeton in a course on Dostoevski given by the critic, R.P. Blackmur. After receiving his M.A. from Harvard, he taught Creative Writing at Williams College in Massachusetts. He recently gave a writing course in London for the American Institute of Foreign Studies.

His first novel, *The Reunion*, was published by The New International Library Inc., and sold very well.

His second novel, *The Lion's Share*, was a fictional account of his experience in the "Battle of the Bulge." This book sold over 6500 copies and is now in its fourth revised edition, published by Avranches Press, 1700 Cheryl Way, Aptos, California 95003.